Autumn
Publishing

Published in 2017
by Autumn Publishing
Cottage Farm
Sywell
NN6 0BJ
www.igloobooks.com

LEO002 0517
2 4 6 8 10 9 7 5 3 1
ISBN 978-1-78810-668-9

The publisher would like to thank Alamy for permission to use the following
images: page 8 (left), ArteSub / Alamy Stock Photo; 10 (left), Nature Picture
Library / Alamy Stock Photo; 11 (bottom), WaterFrame / Alamy Stock Photo; 12
(centre), Alan Skyrme / Alamy Stock Photo; 12 (top), john t. fowler / Alamy Stock
Photo; 12 (centre), blickwinkel / Alamy Stock Photo; 17 (centre), blickwinkel
/ Alamy Stock Photo; 17 (bottom), Minden Pictures / Alamy Stock Photo; 18
(top), All Canada Photos / Alamy Stock Photo; 28 (bottom), Juniors Bildarchiv
GmbH / Alamy Stock Photo; 28 (centre), Mircea Costina / Alamy Stock Photo; 29
(bottom), Alamy Stock Photo. All other images provided by iStockphoto.com.

Cover designed by Richard Sykes
Interiors designed by Starry Dog Books

Printed and manufactured in China

OVER 100

FACTS FOR KIDS
DANGEROUS ANIMALS

Autumn
Publishing

Sharks

FACT 1 Sharks are ancient killers. These toothy fish have prowled the seas since before the time of the dinosaurs.

Bull shark

FACT 2 Bull sharks live in shallow waters near beaches, and often encounter humans. They have an immensely powerful bite.

FACT 3 Sharks can detect a tiny trace of blood in the ocean and follow it to its source.

FACT 4 Tiger sharks are often found with metal and plastic in their stomachs.

Tiger shark

FACT 5 Sharks mostly try to stay away from people, and only attack them by mistake.

FACT 6 Sharks have around 15 rows of teeth in their jaws.

Shark's jaws

FACT 7 Some sharks are dying out because they are killed by humans.

Great white shark

FACT 8 The great white shark can grow up to 6 m (20 ft) long. That's as long as a large van.

FACT 9 The largest shark of all, Megalodon, lived 20 million years ago. It grew to three times the size of a great white.

Great white tooth

Megalodon tooth

Underwater Giants

The sea is home to the largest animals on Earth. Some are harmless, others are fierce hunters.

Giant squid live in the ocean depths. They grab fish with tentacles up to 10 m (33 ft) long. That's twice as long as a car.

The colossal squid is even larger than the giant squid. It grows up to 14 m (46 ft) long.

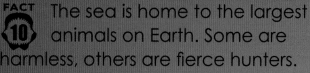

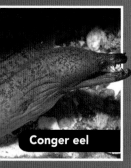

FACT 13

Conger eels are fish with snake-like bodies and super-sharp teeth.

Conger eel

Killer whale

The killer whale, or orca, is a sleek hunter. It can launch itself onto beaches to grab resting seals.

Human   Sperm whale

Sperm whale

FACT 15 Sperm whales can grow to 16 m (52 ft) long, or the length of a large truck. They battle and eat giant squid.

FACT 16 Sperm whales dive more than 2 km (1.2 miles) beneath the waves to hunt, and can hold their breath for 90 minutes.

Giant squid

FACT 17 Walrus tusks can grow up to 90 cm (3 ft) long, or longer than a man's arm.

FACT 18 Walruses can weigh up to 1,500 kg (3,300 lb), or as much as a large car. They have been known to kill polar bears.

Walrus

Poisonous
Sea Creatures

FACT 19 Jellyfish drift through the sea, tangling prey in their long, stinging tentacles.

FACT 20 The box jellyfish is the most dangerous jellyfish in the world. Its sting can kill a human in minutes.

Box jellyfish

Portuguese man o' war

FACT 21 The floating Portuguese man o' war has stinging tentacles up to 30 m (100 ft) long. That's as long as two large trucks.

FACT 22 Scorpion fish have venom-coated spines in their fins.

FACT 23 Some scorpion fish hide on the seabed waiting for prey. Swimmers who tread on them suffer painful stings.

Scorpion fish

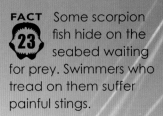

FACT 24 The blue-ringed octopus would fit in your hand, but its venomous bite can kill.

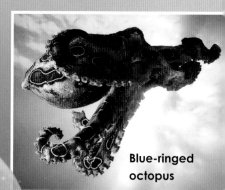

Blue-ringed octopus

FACT 25 Stingrays drift along the seabed. Their tails are equipped with venomous spines to stab attackers.

Stingray

FACT 26 Stingray venom rarely kills humans, but their long, barbed spines can cause dangerous injuries.

FACT 27 Cone snails use venomous darts to defend themselves and kill their prey. Divers who pick them up get a nasty surprise.

Cone snail

Insects

FACT 28 Some insects have powerful bites and stings that they use to drive off or kill attackers.

FACT 29 Asian giant hornets are the world's largest wasps. Their fearsome stings are longer than an ant's whole body.

Asian giant hornet

Asian giant hornet

Adult hand

FACT 30 Parasitic wasps inject eggs into caterpillars and spiders. When the eggs hatch, the host is eaten from the inside.

FACT 31 Bombardier beetles spray attackers with boiling toxic vapour.

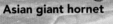

Bombardier beetle

FACT 32 The tiny hairs on the furry puss caterpillar are venomous. If touched, they give a very painful sting.

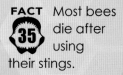

Furry puss caterpillar

FACT 33 Africanised bees are also known as killer bees. They may have killed more than 1,000 people since the 1960s.

FACT 34 Bees sting attackers to drive them away from their hive.

Killer bee

FACT 35 Most bees die after using their stings.

FACT 36 Assassin bugs kill their prey by injecting venom through a long, sharp tube, like a giant fang.

Assassin bug

Spiders and Scorpions

FACT 37 All spiders have venomous fangs for killing prey, but only a few are strong enough to bite humans.

Brazilian wandering spider

FACT 38 The venom from some scorpions is used to make medicine.

FACT 39 The Brazilian wandering spider likes to hide in shoes, clothes and boxes, and its bite can be deadly.

FACT 40 Scorpions have venomous stings in their tails that they use to kill prey.

Funnel-web spider

FACT 41 The world's most poisonous spider is the funnel-web from Australia.

Tarantula

FACT 42 Tarantulas have fangs up to 4 cm (1.5 in) long. However, their bites are rarely dangerous to people.

FACT 43 The Goliath bird-eating spider is the world's largest. Its legs can stretch right across a dinner plate.

Scorpion

Black widow

FACT 44 The black widow spider is often said to be the most venomous, but its bite rarely kills people.

Snakes

FACT 45 Snakes are thought to kill around 120,000 people a year. That's more than any other animal.

FACT 46 Like most animals, snakes stay away from humans. They only bite when they feel scared or trapped.

FACT 47 Sea snakes such as kraits sometimes rest in boats. Their venom is very dangerous.

Sea krait

FACT 48 Rattlesnakes have rattles at the ends of their tails. They shake them to warn other animals not to get too close.

Rattlesnake

FACT 49 Rattlesnake poison is very dangerous to humans. The victim must be given an antidote very soon after being bitten.

Human | **Reticulated python**

FACT 50 Reticulated pythons can grow up to three times the length of a human adult.

FACT 51 Pythons coil around their prey and squeeze them to death.

Anaconda

FACT 52 The heaviest snake is the anaconda. It can weigh more than an adult human.

FACT 53 Spitting cobras squirt venom to blind attackers. They can hit a target 2 m (6.6 ft) away.

Spitting cobra

Crocodiles
and Lizards

FACT 54 Crocodiles kill more people around the world than any other animal, apart from snakes.

Alligator

FACT 55 Crocodiles and alligators hide in shallow water. They grab prey with their teeth, then drown it underwater.

FACT 56 Alligators live in China and America. They are close relatives of crocodiles.

FACT 57 The saltwater crocodile is the largest reptile on Earth, weighing as much as a small car.

FACT 58 Saltwater crocodiles have the strongest bite of any animal alive today.

Saltwater crocodile

FACT 59 The Komodo dragon is the world's largest lizard. It can weigh more than an adult person.

FACT 60 Komodo dragons have saw-like teeth and a powerful bite. They can tackle prey as large as a deer.

Komodo dragon

Gila monster

FACT 61 Gila monsters are lizards with a powerful bite and venomous saliva.

FACT 62 Gila monsters chew their victims to grind venom into them.

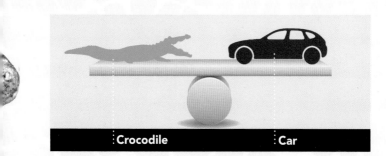

Crocodile   Car

Big Cats

FACT 63 Big cats are powerful predators. They are experts at hunting large animals.

FACT 64 Leopards hunt at night, using their sharp sight and hearing.

Leopard

FACT 65 Leopards often carry their kills into trees to stop other animals stealing them.

FACT 66 The Siberian tiger is the world's largest big cat, weighing up to 300 kg (660 lbs), or as much as five people.

FACT 67 Tigers can kill large animals by clamping their teeth around their necks to strangle them.

FACT 68 There are fewer than 4,000 tigers alive in the world today. Experts fear they may die out.

Tiger

FACT 69 Lions live in groups called prides. Although male lions are bigger, the female lions do the hunting.

FACT 70 In very rare cases, groups of lions have been seen to bring down elephants.

Lion

FACT 71 The cheetah is the fastest land animal. It can run at 110 km/h (70 mph) for short distances.

110 km/h
(70 mph)

44.7 km/h
(27.8 mph)

Cheetah

Dogs, Wolves and Bears

FACT 72 Brown bears eat meat and plants. The largest is the Kodiak bear, which can stand 3 m (10 ft) tall.

Brown bear

Coyote

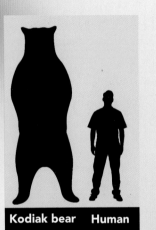

Kodiak bear   Human

FACT 73 Coyotes eat almost anything, from fruit and insects to large bison.

FACT 74 Polar bears live in the icy Arctic. These expert swimmers mostly hunt seals.

FACT 75 Polar bears are the largest land predators. The largest polar bear ever found weighed more than a car.

Polar bear

FACT 76 Spotted hyenas live in Africa. Their powerful bite can crack bones.

FACT 77 Spotted hyenas mostly kill to eat. Striped hyenas mostly feed on already dead animals.

Spotted hyena

FACT 78 Wolves live in packs. Working together, they can bring down a bison.

FACT 79 Grey wolves like to attack animals that are running away.

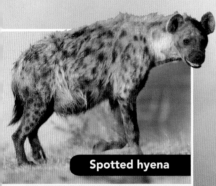

Grey wolves

Dangerous Birds

FACT 80 Ostriches are the world's largest birds. They mostly eat grass, but can kill predators with a kick.

Ostrich

Human Ostrich

FACT 81 Ostriches can't fly, but they can run at 70 km/h (43 mph).

FACT 82 Cassowaries' feet are equipped with dangerous, 10 cm (4 in) long claws.

FACT 83 Cassowaries can grow almost as tall as humans. Like ostriches, they cannot fly.

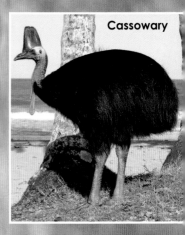
Cassowary

FACT 84 Condors eat the remains of dead animals. They soar up to 5.5 km (3.4 miles) high, scanning the ground for food to eat.

Andean condor

FACT 85 The Andean condor can have a wingspan of more than 3 m (10 ft).

Philippine eagle

FACT 86 The bearded vulture, or lammergeier, cracks open bones with its powerful beak to eat the marrow inside.

FACT 87 Philippine eagles are powerful birds of prey. They can carry off and eat small deer.

FACT 88 Lammergeiers also drop bones from the air onto rocks to crack them open.

Lammergeier

Vicious Vegetarians

African buffalo join together to charge attackers. They can even drive off a pride of lions.

African buffalo can be up to 1.7 m (5.6 ft) tall, or about the height of an adult human.

Hippopotamuses may be vegetarians, but their long, sharp teeth can cause serious injury if they attack.

African buffalo

Hippos can drive away crocodiles, and have been known to sink small boats.

Hippopotamus

FACT 93 Gorillas mostly eat plants and insects, but will attack if threatened. Adult males can weigh up to four times as much as a human.

Gorilla

FACT 94 Elephants kill about the same number of people every year as lions do.

FACT 95 African elephants can weigh up to 7 tonnes. That's more than three large cars.

African elephant

Invisible Killers

FACT 96 Germs kill more people every year than all the animals in this book put together.

FACT 97 Some diseases are spread by animals. Malaria is a deadly disease spread by mosquitoes.

FACT 98 The worst plague in history was the Black Death, which killed up to 100 million people in the 1300s.

Mosquito

FACT 99 The Black Death was spread by fleas living on rats. The rats travelled on trading ships, spreading the disease worldwide.

Rat

FACT 100 Dogs can carry a disease called rabies. People can catch the disease if an infected dog bites them.

Dog

FACT 101 Rabies is very dangerous, but can be cured with a course of injections.

FACT 102 Some water snails carry a parasitic disease called snail fever. This disease kills more than 200,000 people each year in Africa.

FACT 103 Some parasites, such as tapeworms, live inside humans and steal food from inside their bodies.

FACT 104 The largest tapeworm found in a human was over 25 m (80 ft) long. That's longer than a swimming pool.

Tapeworm